A SPECIAL THANK YOU

This book was kindly provided through the support of The Keg Steakhouse + Bar and The Keg Spirit Foundation.

Thanks to their generous contribution, this book is reaching tens of thousands of young people across Canada, and will help inspire a generation of global change-makers.

Proud to support charities that mentor youth through The Keg Spirit Foundation.

My Grandma Follows Me on Twitter
...and other first world problems we're lucky to have

Craig & Marc Kielburger

Me to We
225 Carlton Street
Toronto ON
Canada M5A 2L2
www.metowe.com/books

Distributed by
Greystone Books, D&M Publishers Inc.

Cataloguing data available from Library and Archives Canada
ISBN: 978-1-927435-02-1 (pbk.)
ISBN: 978-1-927435-03-8 (EPDF)

Printed and bound in China by Allied Fortune Printing
Text printed on acid-free paper

*Me to We is committed to reducing the consumption of old-
growth forests in the books it publishes. This book is one step
towards that goal.*

Book design by Frances Data
Illustrations by TurnStyle Imaging

*This book has not been authorized by Twitter, Inc., and there is no
affiliation between the authors and Twitter, Inc., which is the owner of
the Twitter trademark.*

MY GRANDMA FOLLOWS ME ON TWITTER

...AND OTHER FIRST WORLD PROBLEMS WE'RE LUCKY TO HAVE

**CRAIG & MARC KIELBURGER
WITH ED GILLIS**

YOU GOTTA PROBLEM?

We all catch ourselves bemoaning first world woes.

We feel a pang of guilt for complaining when so many others around the world — and in our own communities — have far bigger troubles than ours. Then we move on.

Yet study after study shows that helping others makes us healthier, happier, better-looking* and more grateful for life's simple pleasures. In other words, tackling the world's problems helps us feel better about our own problems.

As founders of Free The Children, we've witnessed some of our world's most serious challenges. When we share them, we're often asked how we cope with the scope of the heartbreak and tragedy. They can be devastating, but our passion to make real change in the world offers blessings every single day.

With this collection of first world problems — some absurd, some we hear every day — we hope to share some laughter, a smile, and a few simple ways to make the world a better place.

Enjoy!

Craig Kielburger   Marc Kielburger

* The better-looking part is pure theory and something we say to convince teenage boys to volunteer.

MY TRIPLE-SCOOP ICE CREAM IS MELTING TOO FAST FOR ME TO CATCH ALL THE SPRINKLES.

DID YOU KNOW?

Canadians consume $2.1 billion in ice cream annually[1] — 11 times more money than we contribute to the Global Fund to Fight AIDS, Tuberculosis and Malaria,[2] and enough to stack scoops halfway to the moon.[3]

WHAT YOU CAN DO

Gather some friends (and lots of spoons), and host an ice cream party fundraiser. A little sweetness can go a long way with Free The Children (**freethechildren.com**): just $60 will provide a mama and her newborn in a developing community with prenatal and postnatal check-ups, as well as vitamins and basic immunizations, for a healthy start.

Mmmmmm...is that mint chocolate chip?

THERE'S NOTHING TO WATCH ON TV BUT POKER TOURNAMENTS AND FOUR DIFFERENT VERSIONS OF *CSI*.

DID YOU KNOW?

The average Canadian spends 17 hours a week watching television[4] and 10 hours worrying about where they left their DNA.

WHAT YOU CAN DO

Take your mind off David Caruso's unnerving stare by volunteering in your community instead. Or, you could write a novelty book like this one, bake a cake, make a YouTube video with friends, or host your own murder-mystery party. (Solving a real-life murder mystery on your own is strongly *not* recommended.)

*Hmmmm...these look like
beaver teeth marks to me, eh?*

I GOT BURNED IN THE TANNING BED AND MY LOBSTER-COLOURED SKIN DOESN'T MATCH MY PROM DRESS.

DID YOU KNOW?

The World Health Organization estimates that using tanning devices before age 30 increases the risk of cancer by 75%.[5]

WHAT YOU CAN DO

Limited sun exposure over weeks (with sunscreen) builds a natural tan and also boosts Vitamin D, which lowers the risk of depression,[6] some cancers and cardiovascular diseases.[7] Find volunteer opportunities that get you outdoors and into the fresh air.

WHENEVER I ORDER A BOOK ONLINE, THE COURIER COMES WHEN I'M STILL AT WORK AND I HAVE TO GO TO THE DELIVERY DEPOT TO GRAB IT.

DID YOU KNOW?

Your local bookstore is probably closer than the next-day delivery outlet tucked in a strip mall on the outskirts of town. The public library is probably even closer, and the books are free!

WHAT YOU CAN DO

They don't wear brown shorts as their uniforms, but the staff at your library love talking about books. Hit them up for recommendations beyond *The Hunger Games*. Or check out a great list of inspiring reads on page 144.

MY GIRLFRIEND STILL HASN'T SUCCESSFULLY CAPTURED MY IDEAL PEANUT BUTTER-TO-JAM RATIO ON MY SANDWICH.

DID YOU KNOW?

Your personal PB-to-J ratio preferences are unique to you — like snowflakes.[8]

WHAT YOU CAN DO

We don't judge on who makes your lunch for you, but paper bags and Saran Wrap are old news: switch to Tupperware or metal containers in a cloth bag for your lunches.

THE TAB ON MY DISPOSABLE COFFEE CUP TORE OPEN TOO FAR AND NOW I'VE SPILLED COFFEE ON MY SHIRT WHILE I WAS DRIVING.

DID YOU KNOW?

Canadians toss 1.6 billion coffee cups a year — resulting in 144 sq. km of lost natural habitat potential.[9]

WHAT YOU CAN DO

Bring a reusable mug with a nice, easy-to-use lid. Try a straw if you can't avoid spilling. And don't drink and drive.

THE PRICE OF GAS IS *ALMOST* TOO HIGH FOR ME TO DRIVE THE FIVE BLOCKS TO THE GYM.

DID YOU KNOW?

Cars account for 63% of total household greenhouse gas emissions and almost 10% of Canada's overall contribution to climate change.[10]

WHAT YOU CAN DO

Use your car less, especially for short distances: walk to the gym, or better yet, jog around the gym and back — a better, cheaper workout!

THEY STILL HAVEN'T INVENTED A PUBLIC FOUNTAIN THAT GIVES OUT JUICE, POP, OR SOMETHING OTHER THAN WATER.

DID YOU KNOW?

11% of the world's population (783 million people) have no access to clean drinking water.[11]

WHAT YOU CAN DO

For $25 (skipping two sodas a month for a year), you can provide a permanent source of clean drinking water for a person overseas through Free The Children (**freethechildren.com**). And it's all zero calories.

I SCORED THE LAST SEAT ON THE BUS, BUT THE BELLY OF THE PREGNANT WOMAN STANDING BESIDE ME KEEPS BUMPING MY HEAD.

DID YOU KNOW?

95% of seniors and pregnant women have sorer feet than yours.[12]

WHAT YOU CAN DO

Give up your seat for someone who needs it — there's a reason there are no reserved bus seats for able-bodied 20-somethings, or people with hockey bags.

MY WORK'S DENTAL PLAN REFUSED TO COVER MY GOLD-AND-DIAMOND GRILLZ.

DID YOU KNOW?

Only one third of non-unionized Canadian workers have work-related medical, dental, life insurance or pension benefits.[13] We're not sure about Nelly, Lil Wayne or Flavor Flav.

WHAT YOU CAN DO

Support companies known for being good employers (**canadastop100.com**). We'll let your BF/GF decide on the grillz.

NEVER MIND THE PELICANS — THE OIL SPILL IN THE GULF OF MEXICO TANKED MY BP STOCKS.

DID YOU KNOW?

Socially-responsible investment (SRI) funds are outperforming the industry average in all eight major asset classes over one-, three-, five- and 10-year returns.[14]

WHAT YOU CAN DO

Talk to family and friends about SRI funds and learn more about how to align your values with future investments through the Social Investment Organization (**socialinvestment.ca**).

THE HOMELESS GUY OUTSIDE MY OFFICE IS SO FRIENDLY THAT I FEEL BAD FOR IGNORING HIM EVERY DAY.

DID YOU KNOW?

Our friend, 17-year-old homelessness advocate Hannah Taylor, who inspired Hannah's Place Emergency Shelter in Winnipeg, says the greatest gift to give a homeless person is to acknowledge that you see them.

WHAT YOU CAN DO

Start with a smile or "Good morning." If you choose not to give, it's okay to simply say "sorry" or "best wishes." Or, take part in "We Won't Rest" (**freethechildren.com/wewontrest**) to raise awareness and take action on homelessness and poverty.

Nice tie, dude.

*Thank you!
FINALLY someone
notices!*

I'M STARVING AND THE FAST FOOD RESTAURANT ACROSS THE STREET DOESN'T DELIVER.

DID YOU KNOW?

40% of Canadian seniors don't get enough calories and protein on a daily basis.[15]

WHAT YOU CAN DO

Volunteer for Meals on Wheels and help a senior in your community have healthy meals every day (**mealcall.org**). Or, deliver one jumbo-large size fast food meal combo that provides enough calories for a week, but we don't recommend this option.

I NEED A NEW TV BECAUSE MY 50" 1080P WIDESCREEN RESOLUTION ISN'T CRYSTAL CLEAR ENOUGH TO SEE THE UVULA* OF THIS YEAR'S *AMERICAN IDOL* CONTESTANTS.

DID YOU KNOW?

More than 140,000 tonnes of e-waste accumulates in Canadian landfills each year. That's equal to the weight of 1½ times the CN tower.[16]

WHAT YOU CAN DO

If possible, settle for having the hockey players on your screen slightly less than life-size until your old TV actually conks out.

* Otherwise known as the "dangling thing at the back of your throat."

MY COTTAGE DOESN'T HAVE INTERNET SO I CAN'T UPDATE MY FACEBOOK TO TELL EVERYONE I'M AT THE COTTAGE.

DID YOU KNOW?

The average Canadian surfs the Internet 45 hours a month,[17] mostly posting wildly glamorous party pictures of themselves or watching videos of rodents on water-skis.

WHAT YOU CAN DO

Enjoy a weekend away reconnecting with nature and your family. Hitting social media withdrawal? Shout out "Like!" every time you see something interesting.

THEY REPLACED THE BACON-CHEESE-AND-GRAVY FRIES IN THE CAFETERIA WITH CARROTS AND HUMMUS.

DID YOU KNOW?

Worldwide, 195 million children suffer from malnutrition.*[18]

WHAT YOU CAN DO

Fundraise or donate $500 to Free The Children's Healthy Lunch Program (**freethechildren.com/gift**), providing a six-month lunch program for an entire class, and help ensure that children do not go hungry while they learn.[19]

* Yeah, it's the same "starving children" argument your parents used when you were little. Now eat your carrots.

I DON'T LIKE WHAT MY PARENTS COOK FOR ME, BUT I DON'T WANT TO GET A JOB TO BUY MY OWN FOOD.

DID YOU KNOW?

Close to one million Canadians rely on food banks every month — and 38% are children.[20]

WHAT YOU CAN DO

On Halloween take part in "We Scare Hunger"[21] (**freethechildren.com/wescarehunger**) collecting non-perishable items for local food banks.

I'M PROCRASTINATING GOING TO THE DENTIST BECAUSE I HAVEN'T FLOSSED AND I DON'T WANT A LECTURE FROM THE HYGIENIST.

DID YOU KNOW?

17% of Canadians avoid dental visits due to cost.[22] Of those who do go to the dentist, 16.5% decline recommended care because of costs.

WHAT YOU CAN DO

You really should floss — dentists have started giving away widescreen TVs to patients who floss regularly.[23] And while you're out buying floss, pick up a few extra toothbrushes and donate them to your local food bank.

MY NAIL CHIPPED AN HOUR AFTER MY $100 MANI-PEDI.

DID YOU KNOW?

Many brands of nail products contain chemicals like formaldehyde, toluene and phthalates that can be hazardous to your health and that of your offspring and the salon workers who breathe them in every day.

WHAT YOU CAN DO

Opt for any number of non-toxic nail polishes from an eco-salon[24] like Vancouver's *She to Shic* or Toronto's *Bloor West Organic Spa* — or Dior's lipstick Nude "*Grège*" n°169, endorsed by Natalie Portman who donates all proceeds to Free The Children's scholarships for girls' secondary education in Kenya.

MY WAITRESS SUBSTITUTED MY PENNE FOR ROTINI, MY ALFREDO FOR ROSÉ, AND MY PORTOBELLO FOR SHIITAKE LIKE I ASKED, BUT SHE PUT MY ORANGE VINAIGRETTE ON THE SALAD INSTEAD OF ON THE SIDE. THERE GOES HER TIP!

DID YOU KNOW?

55% of all full-time wait staff make less than $20,000 per year,[25] working long hour, holidays and weekends.

WHAT YOU CAN DO

Smile at your server, be friendly and tip well. You never know! If you haven't waited tables yourself, you might one day work in restaurants, to save for school, travel or more. Karma's cheap at 15%.

I'M TRYING TO TEXT MY FRIENDS WHILE I'M DRIVING, BUT I KEEP GETTING GREEN LIGHTS.

DID YOU KNOW?

Almost 3/4 of Canadian commuters drive alone,[26] and 8 out of 10 car accidents are caused by distracted driving.[27]

WHAT YOU CAN DO

Carpool, bike-pool or take transit to work with friends and have real-time, in-person conversations — you can still say "LOL" and "happy face" at the end of your sentences.

I HAD TO BUY AN EXTRA BAG OF CHEESIES TO GET TO $5 SO I COULD USE INTERAC AT THE CORNER STORE.

DID YOU KNOW?

On average, businesses pay 19 cents for each Interac purchase, and between 2% - 4% of the total sale for every credit card purchase.[28]

WHAT YOU CAN DO

Pay cash at your local independent small business, and make an instant new friend behind the counter.

SOMEOEN TRUNED OFF MY WORD PROCESSERS SPELL-CHEQUE, AND NOW I RAELIZE I TYPE VREYPORLY AND HAVE FORGOTEN HWO TO SPEL.

DID YOU KNOW?

Boosting the literacy skills of Canadians with the lowest comprehension could get 84,000 people off social assistance and save $500 million a year.[29]

WHAT YOU CAN DO

Volunteer at a school, library or local community centre to tutor younger kids and help them improve their reading and writing skills.

Ah carp. Stoopidthnig.

I NEED A NEW CELL PHONE BECAUSE I WANT TO DOWNLOAD THE APP TO LOCATE THE NEAREST POUTINE STAND.

DID YOU KNOW?

Although 96% of the materials in an average mobile device are recyclable, only 12% of used cell phones in Canada are recycled.[30] The more than 10 million cell phones we trash annually could stretch side-by-side on the TransCanada Highway from Winnipeg to Regina.

WHAT YOU CAN DO

When you upgrade, recycle your old phone at one of thousands of sites across Canada, via **recyclemycell.ca**.

SOMEONE IS KNOCKING ON THE STALL DOOR, BUT I CAN'T SEEM TO TRIP THE MOTION SENSOR ON THE PUBLIC AUTO-FLUSH TOILET.

DID YOU KNOW?

While Canadians collectively flush one trillion litres of clean water every year,[31] 2.5 billion people worldwide live without adequate sanitation facilities.[32]

WHAT YOU CAN DO

Purchase a low-flow toilet or place a two-litre bottle in the back of your current toilet. Or fundraise for latrine-building in a developing country[33] — like the Scouts who will put a purple toilet on your friend's lawn for $15, and will "pass it on" to another lawn of their choice for another $15.

MY HAIR GETS TOO MESSY WHEN I CRUISE TOP-DOWN IN MY CONVERTIBLE.

DID YOU KNOW?

Nobody sees your mop under a bike helmet. And when you remove it, they're too busy checking out your healthy bod with the fitness-level equivalent of someone 10 years younger, your happier mental state, your lower triglycerides and blood pressure, and your two-year-longer life expectancy to notice your helmet head.[34]

WHAT YOU CAN DO

Get a handlebar mirror for your bike — for safety and to tidy up your mop before making your Steve McQueen stylish entrance.

MY BOSS IS TOTALLY MAKING ME WEAR MORE 'FLARE' WHILE WAITING TABLES. PINS, BUTTONS, ALL OVER THE PLACE. MAKES ME LOOK LIKE A CHRISTMAS TREE!

DID YOU KNOW?

Almost one billion people worldwide live on less than $1.25 a day.[35] Wearing buttons with meaning and message can help raise awareness while also raising money for a cause.

WHAT YOU CAN DO

Order your *Love is…* buttons through "We are Love" (**freethechildren.com/wearelove**) and sell them as a fundraiser. Kids everywhere will want to rock this flare, and, more importantly, all proceeds will support Free The Children's Adopt a Village communities around the world.

MY TEAM JUST GOT KNOCKED OUT OF THE PLAYOFFS AND I'M DEAD LAST IN MY HOCKEY POOL.

DID YOU KNOW?

No complaining. We're from Toronto, where our Maple Leafs can go nearly a decade between playoff appearances.

WHAT YOU CAN DO

Hug a Leafs fan (we all know at least one — even if they won't publicly admit it).

I EMPTY MY BANK ACCOUNT EVERY MONTHS ON CLOTHES EVERY MONTH TO KEEP UP WITH TRENDS.

DID YOU KNOW?

Recent immigrants and people with troubled lives often struggle to get good jobs because they lack decent interview clothes.

WHAT YOU CAN DO

Rally your community to donate women's business attire to Dress For Success (**dressforsuccess.org**), or men's suits at **careergear.org**.

MY PARENTS DON'T GET ME. THEY THINK I'M ALWAYS ON FACEBOOK AND UPLOADING PHOTOS TO INSTAGRAM. THERE'S SO MUCH MORE TO ME AND MY LIFE!

DID YOU KNOW?

You're not the only one whose unique attributes may go unnoticed. There are numerous First Nations contributions to contemporary society, such as canoes, the medicine in painkillers like aspirin, and growing practices for foods such as corn, beans, squash and potatoes.[36]

WHAT YOU CAN DO

Educate yourself, and educate others about Aboriginal history, culture and traditions through "We Stand Together" (**freethechildren.com/westandtogether**).

THE GUY I HIRED TO PLAY *WORLD OF WARCRAFT* FOR ME WHILE I'M AT WORK LOST ALL MY HONOUR POINTS, AND NOW I CAN'T BUY THE DEADLY GLADIATOR'S CLOAK OF TRIUMPH.

DID YOU KNOW?

On average, gamers spend more than 13 hours each week playing video games,[37] while adolescent gamers spend 30% less time reading, 34% less time doing homework,[38] and 75% less time dating than non-gamers.[39]

Oh great, how am I supposed to slay Emalon the Storm Watcher with a critical strike rating of 60 percent?

WHAT YOU CAN DO

Discover new adventures and lifelong friends (instead of virtual ones) at the annual Take Action Camp (**metowe. com/camp**). You'll learn leadership skills to change the world, while having an epic time.

MY ONLINE DATING SERVICE MATCHED ME WITH ANOTHER WINNER WHO MISSPELLED THE WORD "INTELLIGENT" IN HIS PROFILE.

DID YOU KNOW?

Women in many developing countries are forced to become teen brides: one in three girls is married before age 18, and one in seven before age 15.[40]

WHAT YOU CAN DO

Hope for a better future comes with holistic development solutions that include empowering women. Make a donation to Free The Children's Alternative Income programs (**freethechildren.com/gift**) in the form of a small business loan for a woman.

Thanks for the poem, but I think "affection"
starts with an 'a', not an 'in',
and it's supposed to have two 'f's'.

I'M ALWAYS RUNNING OUT OF HANGERS — WHERE DOES ONE KEEP A FLEET OF PLANES THESE DAYS?

DID YOU KNOW?

1) Airplane hangars are spelled with an "a." 2) The average family of four generates more greenhouse gases on one transatlantic flight than in all other activities over a year.[41]

WHAT YOU CAN DO

For the 99.99% of us without a Lear Jet, take a "staycation" closer to home, and discover all the incredible adventures your city or province has to offer.

THE SUNSHINE IS SO BRIGHT THAT I CAN'T SEE THE MOVIE ON MY TABLET.

DID YOU KNOW?

Prince Rupert, B.C., averages 240 rainy days and 115 days a year with no glimpse of sun at all.[42] Alert, Nunavut, has no glimpse of natural light except for a few minutes at midday for 1.5 months every winter.[43]

WHAT YOU CAN DO

Push your screen-time to night-time and enjoy the sun. Bring a rain jacket when you visit Prince Rupert, and your tablet to Alert in December.

WHEN I WALK, THE
LOOSE CHANGE IN
MY POCKET MAKES
ME SOUND LIKE A
TAMBOURINE.

DID YOU KNOW?

2.6 billion people live on less than $2 a day, and 879 million live on less than $1 a day.[44]

WHAT YOU CAN DO

Donate the change. Take part in "We Create Change" (**freethechildren.com/wecreatechange**) and turn your small change into big impact. Your donation can be dropped off at RBC branches to support education projects around the world.

MY FACEBOOK NEWS FEED IS SO FULL OF INVITES THAT I MISSED MY BFF'S BIRTHDAY.

DID YOU KNOW?

There's at least one person in your school/office who feels like they have no friends.

WHAT YOU CAN DO

Use your superstar social status for good: say "Hi" to the kid/co-worker that everyone else ignores, or better yet, invite them into your group. If your Facebook events are overflowing, you've got enough Cool Capital* to spare.

Accumulated cool points: if you lose a few, you've still got loads of cool to work with. Like life-essence points in video games… okay so maybe we were two of those kids with no friends.

MY GRANDMA FOLLOWS ME ON TWITTER.

DID YOU KNOW?

99.9% of grandmas would suffer a health crisis if they saw what you post on your social media of choice — or at least skip your plate in dealing out fresh apple cobbler on your next visit.

WHAT YOU CAN DO

Show your grandma some love, and stay in touch with a handwritten update letter. And save your embarrassing diary entries for Facebook with privacy settings — grandma's happy and you get more than 140 characters.

I SPENT MY WHOLE BIRTHDAY READING THE BIRTHDAY GREETINGS FROM MY 1,200 FACEBOOK FRIENDS.

DID YOU KNOW?

Many children in developing countries don't celebrate birthdays because they don't know the date of their birth, and so have few legal rights in their country.

WHAT YOU CAN DO

On your birthday, call your Mom to say thanks (we celebrate you, but she did all the work). Then, pay forward your good fortune by performing a random act of kindness for a stranger.

MY TEACHER WON'T LET ME HAND IN A BOOK REPORT ON *ROLLING STONE'S* TEN GREATEST DRUMMERS OF ALL TIME.

DID YOU KNOW?

They only accept those at Dave Grohl's School of Rock![45]

WHAT YOU CAN DO

Convince your English teacher to let you study enlightening classics like *Oliver Twist* or *The Grapes of Wrath*, or inspiring real-life stories of young people like Robin Wiszowaty's *My Maasai Life* or Spencer West's *Standing Tall*. See page 144 for more inspiring reads.

I'M 40 AND MY PARENTS STILL GIVE ME CHRISTMAS GIFTS FROM SANTA CLAUS.

DID YOU KNOW?

If your parents think you've been a good kid they're obviously not tracking you on Twitter like grandma does.

WHAT YOU CAN DO

You may not get Ryan Gosling tied in a bow, but you can order him on a card! Check out the "Ryan Gosling Was Too Busy to be Gift Wrapped" greeting card along with the full collection of First World Problems cards through Me to We (**metowe.com/cards**). The purchase of each card helps deliver a specific gift to a child or family in a developing country.

Dear Santa, I've been good all year.
Please bring: 1. A new pilates mat.
2. Desperate Housewives box set.
3. Ryan Gosling wrapped in a bow.

THEY INTERRUPTED THE FINALE OF *SURVIVOR* WITH NEWS ABOUT AN EARTHQUAKE SOMEWHERE.

DID YOU KNOW?

They wouldn't even interrupt the finale of *Survivor* for the Emergency Broadcast System.

WHAT YOU CAN DO

Donate your spare blankets and canned food to local homeless shelters, your spare cash to overseas disaster-relief organizations, or your spare blood through Canadian Blood Services (**bloodservices.ca**).

MY KID'S HOCKEY SCHEDULE IS SO DEMANDING THAT WE PRE-BOOK SPAGHETTI NIGHT TWO MONTHS IN ADVANCE.

DID YOU KNOW?

A third of Canadian kids can't afford to play organized sports.[46] Among them is the one who would have led the Leafs to win the 2019 Stanley Cup.

WHAT YOU CAN DO

Donate your old hockey equipment through Restore Hockey (**restorehockey.org**), or check whether your local sporting-goods store sells used equipment at reduced rates for those in need.

I MADE WAY TOO MUCH BEAN CHILI AND NOW MY TASTE BUDS ARE NUMB FROM EATING IT FOR BREAKFAST, LUNCH *AND* SUPPER.

DID YOU KNOW?

Chances are one of your friends or neighbours doesn't have the ability to prepare their own meals — because of illness, hectic schedule, recent birth or death in the family, or other reasons.

WHAT YOU CAN DO

Get to know your neighbours. And when you have leftovers (by accident or on purpose), package up a meal-sized container for someone who would appreciate your home-cooked delight — in modest quantities.

I FOUND THE ROOM WITH ALL-YOU-CAN-PLAY X-BOX ON MY ALL-INCLUSIVE CRUISE AND MISSED ALL THE STOPS.

DID YOU KNOW?

A large cruise ship on a one-week voyage generates 210,000 gallons of human sewage, 25,000 gallons of oily bilge water, and more than 130 gallons of hazardous waste.[47]

WHAT YOU CAN DO

Who needs the Greek Islands? Our Home-and-Native-Land could fit 80 Greeces, four Caribbeans or all of Europe (well, minus Russia).

THE NEW GUY AT WORK TAKES HIS DAILY PEE BREAK AT THE SAME TIME AS ME. EVERY. SINGLE. DAY.

DID YOU KNOW?

Statistically speaking, in an office with 120 or more employees, your pee time is bound to coincide with someone else's on any given day.[48]

WHAT YOU CAN DO

Help make new co-workers feel welcome by introducing yourself (outside of the washroom is less awkward) and inviting them to join your circle of friends for lunch.

I GOT A CRUMMY GIFT FOR LAST YEAR'S CHRISTMAS EXCHANGE, BUT MY FAMILY REFUSES TO RAISE THE SPENDING LIMIT ABOVE $50.

DID YOU KNOW?

With over 600,000 Canadian children (1 in 10) living below the poverty line,[49] many families can't afford gifts for the holiday season.

WHAT YOU CAN DO

Instead of exchanging gifts, pitch-in as a family to give a happier Christmas to a needy family through a local service organization. Bonus: no awkward "Of course I like the sweater you knitted, Aunt Bea…" moments.

MY ED HARDY* T-SHIRTS COST $60 EACH SO I COULD ONLY BUY THREE.

DID YOU KNOW?

The cotton in one regular cotton T-shirt requires a third of a pound of pesticides and uses 1,170 litres of water.[50]

WHAT YOU CAN DO

Buy organic cotton, hemp or bamboo T-shirts at **metowestyle.com** — sweatshop-free, made-in-Canada, and if you buy a tee, they'll plant a tree. And they don't cost $60!

Insert "Polo Ralph Lauren," if you grew up in the '80s. It's tough to keep up with trends.

MY ABILITY TO CONSISTENTLY SCORE OVER A MILLION POINTS ON *ANGRY BIRDS* ISN'T DEEMED A SUFFICIENTLY MARKETABLE SKILL TO LAND A FULL-TIME JOB.

DID YOU KNOW?

Your workplace may not appreciate your more eclectic talents, but non-profit organizations need volunteers with a wider range of skills and interests than you'd think!

No job for you, and may I suggest anger management class.

| WHAT YOU CAN DO |

Join **We365.com** to find the causes you care about and how you can take action. Build a portfolio of social good for work, university or scholarship applications by joining an online community where you can turn your passion into action.

I RAN OUT OF HOT WATER IN THE SHOWER AFTER ONLY 45 MINUTES.

DID YOU KNOW?

Of the more than 1,500 Olympic-sized swimming pools of water that Canadians use every day, almost 1,000 would be filled with hot water,[51] accounting for over 20% of our total energy use.[52]

WHAT YOU CAN DO

Install a low-flow shower head, adopt a staggered shower (save water by shampooing and soaping with the shower tap off).

IF I WALK TO THE NEARBY POLLING STATION TO VOTE IN THE ELECTION I WILL MISS VOTING FOR MY FAVOURITE *CANADIAN IDOL* SINGER.

DID YOU KNOW?

2.6 billion people lack democratic rights.[53] And if you don't vote, you're not allowed to complain about anything that our government does.

WHAT YOU CAN DO

If you're worried about long line-ups, vote at advance polls, then tell your friends you voted for the most objectionable choice that will infuriate them, prompting them to also vote in order to cancel you out.

MY $6 GLUTEN-FREE, NUT-FREE, DAIRY-FREE, SOY-BASED MUFFIN WAS NOT BAKED FRESH THIS MORNING, SO I TOOK ONE BITE AND THREW IT OUT.

DID YOU KNOW?

Toronto alone throws out food equivalent to the weight of 35,000 African elephants every year.[54]

WHAT YOU CAN DO

Before you toss old food, consider creative ways to salvage it: blackened bananas go great in banana bread, mushy tomatoes in pasta sauce, and rotten eggs for that co-worker who keeps stealing your parking spot.

I'M OUT OF PERFUME SO I'VE GOTTA SMELL LIKE *NOTHING* ALL DAY.

DID YOU KNOW?

Every morning the average woman dabs 12 personal care products on her face and body, exposing herself to 126 chemicals. And let's not forget one in seven Canadians have a breathing problem affected by chemicals in scented products.[55]

WHAT YOU CAN DO

Buy from **TheGreenBeautyGuide.com**, your local health-food store — or make your own. See endnote for recipes with coconut oil, corn starch and baking soda (nope, this isn't a joke).[56]

MY LAPTOP BATTERY DIED IN THE MIDDLE OF STREAMING *GREY'S ANATOMY*. GOTTA GRAB A CORD WHILE WONDERING WHETHER OR NOT DEREK WILL FORGIVE MEREDITH THIS TIME.

DID YOU KNOW?

Derek's just a grumpy pouter with fancy hair. He always forgives Meredith.

WHAT YOU CAN DO

Conserve your battery life by unplugging your laptop when fully-charged, recharging only when the battery is completely drained, and removing the battery for extended periods of plug-in time. Then recycle your old batteries at designated locations found at **call2recycle.ca**.

MY AIR CONDITIONING IS TOO COLD BUT MY HOUSEMATE GETS MAD WHEN I LEAVE THE FRONT DOOR OPEN.

DID YOU KNOW?

As much as 25% of your home's heat and cool air escapes via leaky windows[57] — a much higher percentage than teens who sneak out through windows at night or boyfriends who sneak in.

WHAT YOU CAN DO

Do a makeshift energy audit on your home with tips like holding a stick of incense to windows and doors — if the smoke wavers, you're losing heat.[58] Save money and the planet.

I ONLY GET TIME-AND-A-HALF FOR WORKING CANADA DAY.

DID YOU KNOW?

12 million people work in debt bondage, trafficking, and other forms of modern slavery and are denied $20 billion in unpaid earnings.[59]

WHAT YOU CAN DO

PVR the televised Parliament Hill Nickelback concert (or better yet, don't), and make your overtime pay count by buying fair-trade clothing from Me to We Style (**metowestyle.com**).

I'M NOT GETTING ANY RECEPTION ON MY WILDERNESS BACKPACKING TRIP SO I CAN'T CHECK MY BLOG STATS.

DID YOU KNOW?

Protecting wildlife habitat in parks has brought several species back from near-extinction, including whooping cranes, sea otters and Blanding's Turtles.[60]

WHAT YOU CAN DO

Support Canada's parks and invest in your sanity by unplugging, unwinding and going *incommunicado* for a few days in the wilderness. And don't feed the bears.

I MISSED *PRETTY LITTLE LIARS* YESTERDAY – NOW I HAVE TO AVOID TALKING TO MY BFFS UNTIL IT'S ONLINE.

DID YOU KNOW?

More than 1.3 billion people do not have access to electricity,[61] and thus have no idea that "A" is actually Mona and Toby! OMG!

WHAT YOU CAN DO

Preserve the planet by saving electricity: host a weekly viewing party at your house (red hoods and creepy text messages optional). Think of it as car pooling, but for TV.

I'M DIZZY FROM LICKING THE ENVELOPES OF THE CHRISTMAS CARDS I JUST MAILED TO MY 100 CLOSEST FAMILY AND FRIENDS.

DID YOU KNOW?

Canadians buy 185 million Christmas and New Years greeting cards every year[62] — enough to fill a football field over four feet high.

WHAT YOU CAN DO

Order Me to We greeting cards (**metowe.com/cards**). Each card gives a gift to a child overseas, such as clean drinking water.[63] You can also create your own card. Our favourite message: "May you live to be so old that your driving terrifies people."

MY FAVOURITE CHOCOLATE BAR HAS GRADUALLY BECOME MORE EXPENSIVE YET HALF THE SIZE IT USED TO BE.

DID YOU KNOW?

Over 100,000 child labourers work in the cocoa fields of Cote d'Ivoire, the source of 40% of the world's chocolate.[64]

WHAT YOU CAN DO

Visit the Me to We store (**metowe.com/store**) in Toronto to buy fair-trade chocolate like Cocoa Camino[65] and feel free to send us some too!*

* FYI: Caramel crunch is our favourite, and our mailing address is inside the front cover.

HAVING FOUR BATHROOMS MEANS HAVING TO CLEAN FOUR TOILETS.

DID YOU KNOW?

A Canadian family uses 20 to 40 litres of toxic cleaning products a year — including carcinogens, reproductive toxins, and endocrine-disputing chemicals that can affect both humans and wildlife.[66]

WHAT YOU CAN DO

Switch to natural home cleaning with vinegar added to baking soda: for your sink, toilet, clogged drain, or fifth-grade volcano science project. See endnote for some great recipes.[67]

MY WIFE IS TIRING OF MY TRI-ANNUAL BIRTHDAY GIFT ROTATION OF GOLD EARRINGS, THEN NECKLACE, THEN BRACELET... AND SHE SAYS RAPTORS' TICKETS DON'T COUNT AS GIFTS FOR HER.

DID YOU KNOW?

65% of Canadians would be happy receiving an ethical gift for the holidays (73% among women).[68]

WHAT YOU CAN DO

Learn more about Me to We Artisans (**metowe.com/artisans**), which offers jewellery, handbags and accessories handcrafted by women in developing communities to provide them with economic empowerment. And we'll go to Raptors' games with you on your birthday, if you want.

I CAN'T WALK IN TO MY WALK-IN CLOSET FOR THE PILES OF CLOTHES SPILLING OUT.

DID YOU KNOW?

The total amount of textiles thrown into landfills in Canada in a one-year period could build a structure the size of the SkyDome* — three times over![69]

WHAT YOU CAN DO

De-clutter and donate to your local women's or homeless shelter, or a local thrift store that donates all proceeds to a range of local charities.

Apologies to Rogers, but it'll always be "SkyDome" to us.

*I know it's a bit retro, but it's so light and airy.
I couldn't resist!*

MY FRIENDS CAUGHT ME HUMMING *THE BACKYARDIGANS* THEME SONG AND NOW THEY SAY I'M TOO HAPPY TO BE A GOTH.

DID YOU KNOW?

Studies show that a happy brain is more efficient and productive than a stressed or negative one.[70]

WHAT YOU CAN DO

As the great Bobby McFerrin taught us in the 1980s, *Don't Worry, Be Happy.* He never told us how. Happiness guru Shawn Achor recommends re-wiring your brain by writing down three things you're grateful for, and journaling one positive experience every day for three weeks. We recommend random acts of kindness for friends or complete strangers.

THERE'S NO PIZZA JOINT ON THE BEACH IN THIS MEXICAN RESORT TOWN.

DID YOU KNOW?

Tourism is the main export in a third of all developing countries.[71]

WHAT YOU CAN DO

When on vacation, maximize your contribution to the community by choosing locally owned restaurants, tour operators and shops as much as possible. Note: Taco Bell does *not* count.

THE STRAWBERRIES I BUY IN JANUARY LAST HALF AS LONG, TASTE HALF AS GOOD, AND COST TWICE AS MUCH AS THE ONES I BUY IN JULY.

DID YOU KNOW?

The average winter strawberry's trip to Canada is 3,600 km.[72]

WHAT YOU CAN DO

Support your local farmers' markets.[73] Or, subscribe to a weekly community-supported agriculture (CSA) basket — a service that delivers local, farm-fresh produce to your doorstep.[74]

Hola cousin! Off to Canada.
I hear it's lovely in January.

I'VE TAKEN CREDIT FOR MY COLLEAGUES' WORK SO MANY TIMES THAT I'VE BEEN ENCOURAGED TO "COLLABORATE" BY MYSELF FROM NOW ON.

DID YOU KNOW?

75% of people experience an increase in productivity when encouraged to collaborate with others.[75]

WHAT YOU CAN DO

Send, Rafiki Friend Chains (**metowe.com/artisans**) in appreciation to co-workers who have gone the extra mile to make your job easier this year. They'll likely repeat the effort next time you're in need, or even cover for you leaving early for the cottage.

I CAN'T SEE THE WINTER WONDERLAND OUTDOORS BECAUSE MY WINDOWS ARE FOGGED OVER FROM KEEPING IT NICE AND TOASTY INSIDE FOR SHORTS AND T-SHIRTS.

DID YOU KNOW?

If every Canadian turned down their thermostat by two degrees in the winter, we'd cut 5% off our heating bills and 2,200 kilo-tonnes of carbon dioxide a year out of our climate.[76]

WHAT YOU CAN DO

Set your thermostat two degrees higher in the summer and two degrees lower in the winter.

I CAN'T HEAR THE TV OVER THE SOUND OF MY MOM VACUUMING.

DID YOU KNOW?

98% of Canadian teenagers don't know where the "on" switch is located on the family vacuum cleaner.[77]

WHAT YOU CAN DO

Appreciate your mother: learn to vacuum. Studies show that kids who begin household tasks at an early age grow into more well-adjusted adults.[78]

*No Rebecca!
Don't marry Vance again!*

THE DRIVE TO THE GROCERY STORE ISN'T FAR ENOUGH TO WARM UP MY SEAT HEATERS.

DID YOU KNOW?

The average member of a car-sharing program reduces their driving by 50%, which reduces 1.2 tonnes of CO_2 per year. Every shared car replaces six to eight private cars on our roads.[79]

WHAT YOU CAN DO

In a car co-op (**carsharing.ca**): insurance, repairs and even fuel costs are included with membership, saving you cash.[80] Plus, with car-pooling extra bodies in the car means more body heat to defrost the windows.

I WAS WATCHING THE NEW ROBERT PATTINSON MOVIE, AND THIS GIRL WOULDN'T STOP TALKING. R-PATS SHOULD BE APPRECIATED IN SILENCE!

DID YOU KNOW?

More than 121 million primary-school aged children around the world are not in school.[81] Their voices are silenced from poverty, exploitation and a lack of education.

WHAT YOU CAN DO

Take a 24-hour vow of silence by participating in "We are Silent" (**freethechildren.com/wearesilent**). Collect pledges for your silence to make a difference in the lives of children around the world. Don't speak, but you can tweet, post, and share your experience to raise awareness.

I CAN'T GET A DECENT WI-FI SIGNAL IN THE PUBLIC WASHROOM.

DID YOU KNOW?

1) 16% of mobile devices have traces of fecal matter on them.[82]

WHAT YOU CAN DO

Create your personal fundraising page on **We365.com** to support your favourite charity. Invite family and friends to donate in your name on birthdays and other special occasions. But please wait until after washing your hands to check your totals.

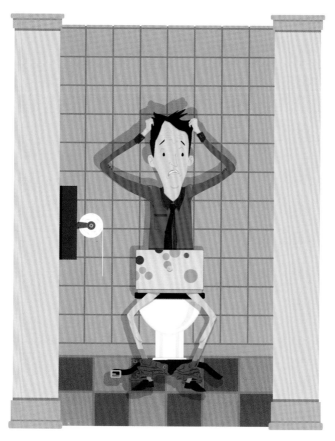

Oh man! What do I do now?

THERE'S AN ANNOYING, CONSTANT BEEPING NOISE IN MY HOUSE BUT I CAN'T FIGURE OUT IF IT'S MY CELL PHONE, MY KOBO, MY DVR, OR MY MICROWAVE.

DID YOU KNOW?

Twilight makes vampires sexy, but vampire power simply sucks your wallet. Standby energy drains 5% - 10% of a home's annual power usage.[83]

WHAT YOU CAN DO

Plug electronic items into a power cord with a convenient one-touch off switch. Or, if you really want to geek out, buy a Kill-a-Watt to measure how much juice your dormant devices are leeching.

Hello? Hello?
Why does it smell like popcorn in here?

I'VE SENT MY FRIEND THREE TEXT MESSAGES IN THE PAST HOUR AND SHE HASN'T RESPONDED TO ANY OF THEM.

DID YOU KNOW?

Canadians send 220 million text messages a day (seven per man, woman and child).[84]

WHAT YOU CAN DO

Text with purpose. Join **We365.com**, an online community for social good. Discover, share, and join with friends in service actions.

*Whoa, dude!
Skateboarding
injury?*

*No.
Serious texting.*

I REFUSE TO BUY NEW HOUSE PLANTS AFTER THEY ALL DIED — AGAIN — DURING MY PRE-EXAMS "STAYCATION" IN THE SCHOOL LIBRARY.

DID YOU KNOW?

Don't feel too badly. Once we actually melted a *plastic* plant by leaving it too close to the stove burner.

WHAT YOU CAN DO

Next time plant outside where Mother Nature helps with the water. Add an extra row of nutritious produce in your own garden for your local food bank (check out **growarow. org** for participating communities across Canada).

MY GROCERY BILL IS SO LONG YOU'D THINK I WAS STOCKPILING FOR THE APOCALYPSE.

DID YOU KNOW?

The paper used for store receipts in North America each year would make a roll long enough to circle the Earth 15 times.[85]

WHAT YOU CAN DO

Opt out of your receipt if you don't need it — resist pressing "print" at the ATM machine. The answer won't change: you're still broke.

I CAN'T FIND A RADIO STATION THAT PLAYS MUSIC INSTEAD OF BAD DJ HUMOUR DURING MY HOUR-LONG MORNING DRIVE TO WORK.

DID YOU KNOW?

Today, more than one million Canadians who want to work are unemployed.[86]

WHAT YOU CAN DO

Download a podcast of music for your commute, including a few oldies as a nod of gratitude to your grandparents, who likely had to get up at 4 a.m., shovel 20-feet of snow, and walk 15 miles uphill (both ways) to get to work selling vacuum cleaners door-to-door.

IT TAKES FOREVER RUNNING THE TAP TO GET THE WATER COLD ENOUGH TO DRINK.

DID YOU KNOW?

In rural Africa, women spend 26% of their day collecting water, often walking five miles to the nearest water source. During dry season, the distance can double.[87]

WHAT YOU CAN DO

Cold water recipe: Shut off faucet when glass is near full. Approach freezer. Remove tray of tiny frozen blocks. Introduce blocks to glass. Stir with finger. Then flip to the endnotes to see how $25 gives a permanent source of clean water to a person overseas, or how to fundraise for a water project to support an entire community.[88]

MY TEAM PEETA SHIRT SHRUNK IN THE WASH AND I HAD TO THROW IT AWAY. I WAS LEANING TOWARD GALE ANYWAY.

DID YOU KNOW?

Canadian clothes dryers collectively consume more electricity than all of Guatemala, Kenya, or 95 other countries[89] — and they cost between $800 and $2,000 over an 18-year life, compared to $30 for a clothes drying rack.[90]

WHAT YOU CAN DO

Save your shirts, the planet and some cash by air-drying your duds. They'll last until you see the final *Hunger Games* film and realize the errors of your choice.*

* Oops! Should we have said "spoiler alert"?

MY BOSS INSISTS THAT I STOP WEARING PYJAMAS ON MY SKYPE CALLS FROM HOME WITH THE BOARD OF DIRECTORS.

DID YOU KNOW?

If one million Canadians worked from home just one day a year, we would save 100 million litres of fuel and 250 million kilograms of CO_2 — that's up to 5,193 cars off the road per year.[91]

WHAT YOU CAN DO

Explore working from home one day a week or more — save commuting time and money. Plus, the dress code is (almost) always casual Fridays.

THE ONLY ITEM LEFT ON MY COUSIN'S WEDDING REGISTRY IS A WOODEN TOILET-PAPER HOLDER... I GOT HIM A MANTEL CLOCK FOR HIS LAST WEDDING.

DID YOU KNOW?

An estimated $19 billion is spent on wedding gift registries in North America every year,[92] and 90% of it will be kept out of guilt instead of utility.[93]

WHAT YOU CAN DO

For the couple who probably has everything, offer a gift in their name to a family that does not: Free The Children (**freethechildren.com/gifts**) is a charitable organization with a "gift" guide to tailor your donation to the happy couple. At $50, the goat is a favourite. At $500, you can provide textbooks for an entire classroom.

MY RIDING LAWN MOWER IS OUT OF GAS, AND MY LAWN IS TOO BIG TO MOW BY FOOT.

─────┤ DID YOU KNOW? ├─────

For every poorly kept yard there's an apartment dweller who dreams of having a vegetable garden.

─────┤ WHAT YOU CAN DO ├─────

Check out **sharingbackyards.com** that connects apartment dwellers with busy homeowners whose untended backyards yearn to be gardened. The grass is always greener…to someone else.

TWO THINGS BUG ME ABOUT MY EXOTIC RESORT: THE SLUMS ON THE DRIVE FROM THE AIRPORT, AND THE LACK OF GRAPE JELLY AT THE BREAKFAST BAR.

DID YOU KNOW?

A volunteer vacation is less relaxing and even less likely to have grape jelly, but you feel better at the end of it.

WHAT YOU CAN DO

For your next vacation, volunteer overseas with Me to We trips (**metowe.com/trips**), and discover meaningful travel in destinations such as Kenya, Ghana, India, Ecuador, the Amazon, Nicaragua and Arizona.[94]

IT'S SO HARD TO VIEW THE TREES THROUGH MY TINY HUMMER H2 WINDOWS.

DID YOU KNOW?

If the tips of tree branches could make a gesture…

WHAT YOU CAN DO

Try a Sunday bike ride instead, join with friends and peddle for a cause, or get adventurous and sign up for a multi-week Otesha bike tour presenting theatre on sustainable consumption across Canada: **otesha.ca**.

I GET NERVOUS WATCHING MY ELDERLY NEIGHBOUR SHOVEL SNOW OFF HIS ROOF.

DID YOU KNOW?

A study by Harvard University demonstrated that after performing a good deed, participants showed stronger willpower, greater physical endurance[95] and fewer signs of being a big jerk.[96]

WHAT YOU CAN DO

Shovel a neighbour's driveway, ask if they need any groceries when you're out at the store, or offer to watch *Matlock* with them.

I STILL DON'T KNOW HOW TO PERFECTLY FOLD MY FITTED BED SHEETS WITH THE ELASTIC CORNERS.

DID YOU KNOW?

In addition to Canada's 300,000 visibly homeless population,[97] nearly 900,000 Canadians stay with friends or family indefinitely due to housing instability.

WHAT YOU CAN DO

Donate gently-used bedding to a local shelter, and/or buy a mattress from a retailer that offers to donate your previous mattress to those in need, like Sleep Country.[98] We promise you'll sleep like a baby.

MY FRIENDS CALL ME A GEEK FOR WATCHING THE NEWS, BUT THEY THINK "ARAB SPRING" IS A ROCK BAND.

DID YOU KNOW?

Only 15% of Canadians pay attention to federal politics.[99]

WHAT YOU CAN DO

You don't have to be an Austrian former bodybuilder and action-movie star to get involved in politics: follow the news, "friend" your MP, volunteer on a campaign, or run for office yourself.

MY 80GB MP3 PLAYER ONLY HOLDS 50 DAYS WORTH OF MUSIC. WHAT IF I'M LOST IN THE WOODS FOR EIGHT WEEKS (IF I EVER DO GO INTO THE WOODS)?

DID YOU KNOW?

In the time it takes you to open the box and charge your new MP3 player, 15 new and better MP3 players will have been released.[100] Admit defeat: you'll never be able to keep up.

WHAT YOU CAN DO

Before you toss that old device, check the endnote for companies that may be able to save your electronics when their warranties expire.[101]

I HAVE 100,000 FREQUENT FLYER MILES, BUT CAN NEVER GET A FLIGHT HOME AT CHRISTMAS.

DID YOU KNOW?

Almost eight trillion miles — enough for 80 million free return flights to Australia — are held by people who save, but don't redeem, their travel perks.[102]

WHAT YOU CAN DO

Why not share your air? Donate your Aeroplan miles (**beyondmiles.aeroplan.com**) to Free The Children, helping inspire and empower more young people to be the change around the world. Or see the change first hand—redeem miles toward a Me to We volunteer trip (**metowe.com/trips**).

I'VE FINISHED READING *MY GRANDMA FOLLOWS ME ON TWITTER*, AND NOW I HAVE TO WAIT MONTHS FOR THE SEQUEL.

DID YOU KNOW?

Look on the bright side: you enjoyed a good laugh while some others may not have been fortunate to find this book.

WHAT YOU CAN DO

Share the love. Don't leave this paperback on your bookshelf. Gift this book to a friend, colleague, or the grumpy guy who needs a pick-me-up. This saves the paper required to print a new one.*

Although if you choose to purchase extra copies for many friends, you are donating to charity and gifting school supplies to children overseas.

ACKNOWLEDGEMENTS

It takes a lot to compile a collection of soft and shameful complaints. But if we explained the saga of the process it might actually qualify as a first world problem. Then we'd have to include it in the main body, and that would require laying out the entire book again. And complaining about that, too, would likely qualify it as a first world problem. (And so on.)

So let's just proceed by simply thanking all of the great folks who contributed their skills, time, advice and inspiration to make this fun book happen.

It all starts with a tip of a Paul Bunyan-sized hat in tribute to the wonderful humour of our dear ol' friend, Ed "I can't stop making chili" Gillis. Without Eddie's funny bone, we'd simply have a collection of helpful yet sobering facts and tips. Thanks to Shelley "Really, I've never read *Twilight*" Page and Sean "Whaddya mean we can't use profanity?" Deasy for their skillful editing. Thanks to Frances "How many times must I pore over the same copy?" Data for her amazing design skills. Special thanks to Marisa "Will you guys decide on sketches already" Antonello for her talents in creating the wonderfully hilarious illustrations (including the crazy-accurate caricature of Ryan Gosling!). Thanks to Marisa "Facts-shmacts" Dametto for her tireless research. And of course to Ryan "I'll be vacationing during production" Bolton for keeping the project together so seamlessly.

We'd particularly love to thank our Free The Children board members for their tireless support, dedication and inspiration. And to the many, many team members across Free The Children and Me to We who offered us their first world problems unwittingly, simply by chatting too loudly around the water cooler.

On a truly sincere note: a warm thank you to the educators, schools, companies and legions of young people across Canada and around the world who make Free The Children possible. And, as always, our deepest and most heartfelt gratitude to our family: Mom, Dad, Roxanne and Lily-Rose for all their love and support.

And thank you for picking up this book and supporting the work of Free The Children.

CRAIG AND MARC KIELBURGER

ENDNOTES

1. The Canadian Dairy Commission, www.cdc-ccl.gc.ca/CDC/index-eng.php?id=3800

2. Canadian HIV/Aids Legal Network, www.marketwire.com/press-release/ngo-leaders-canadas-global-fund-contribution-positive-step-must-be-strengthened-complemented-1323590.htm

3. The price and size of ice-cream scoops varies — we're assuming $1 for a scoop that's 10-centimetre in diameter. Take that, Grade 10 math!

4. Ipsos Reid North America, www.ipsos-na.com/news-polls/pressrelease.aspx?id=4720

5. The World Health Organization.

6. Vitamin D Council, www.vitamindcouncil.org/health-conditions/mental-health-and-learning-disorders/depression/

7. Statistics Canada, www.statcan.gc.ca/pub/82-625-x/2010001/article/11137-eng.htm

8. Scientific study by us. Control group size: us and a couple friends around the office.

9. Be The Change Earth Alliance, www.bethechangeearthalliance.org/youthaction/thefacts (Note: this site miscalculates the conversion from square metres to square kilometres. We've corrected that calculation here.)

10. Statistics Canada, www.statcan.gc.ca/pub/16-001-m/2010012/part-partie1-eng.htm

11. World Health Organization, www.who.int/mediacentre/news/releases/2012/drinking_water_20120306/en/index.html

12. The other five percent would definitely still like to sit.

13. Canadian Labour Congress, www.canadianlabour.ca/about-clc/union-advantage

14. Social Investment Organization, www.socialinvestment.ca/documents/SRI_Funds_Perform_Strongly_SIO_2012.pdf

A great information source on socially responsible investing.

15. Canoe and the MediResource Clinical Team, chealth.canoe.ca/channel_section_details.asp?text_id=1554&channel_id=44&relation_id=48471

16. Shift Recycling, shiftrecycling.com/e-waste.php

17. *The Globe and Mail*, www.theglobeandmail.com/technology/tech-news/canada-tops-globe-in-internet-usage/article551593/

18. *Medecins Sans Frontieres*, www.msf.org/msf/articles/2011/10/food-aid-system-continues-to-fail-malnourished-children.cfm

19. For more alternative gift ideas for all occasions, see the full catalogue online at freethechildren.com/gift

20. Food Banks Canada, www.foodbankscanada.ca/Learn-About-Hunger/About-Hunger-in-Canada.aspx

21. We Scare Hunger takes place on Halloween, October 31st, as thousands take action to scare local hunger and poverty. By trick-or-treating for non-perishable food items instead of just candy, or collecting canned goods at school and in their community, young people support their local food bank and raise awareness. www.freethechildren.com/wescarehunger

22. *CBC Online*, www.cbc.ca/news/health/story/2010/05/10/dental-health-oral-statistics-canada.html

23. No, they haven't. But if you're willing to search all the way in the back of the book for the endnotes, you're not too lazy to start flossing.

24. Vancouver's She to Shic, shetoshic.com or Toronto's Bloor West Organic Spa, bloorwestspa.com

25. Service Canada, www.servicecanada.gc.ca/eng/qc/job_futures/statistics/6453.shtml

26. Statistics Canada, publications.gc.ca/collections/collection_2010/statcan/CS97-561-2006-1-eng.pdf

27. *CTV News*, www.ctv.ca/CTVNews/TopStories/20101004/canada-driving-poll-101004/

28. *CBC*, www.cbc.ca/news/story/2009/04/16/f-cardfees.html

29. Canadian Literacy and Learning Network, www.literacy.ca/content/uploads/2012/03/CLLN-response-federal-budget-2012.pdf

30. The Source, www.thesource.ca/sitelets/mobilerecycle/

31. Environment Canada, www.ec.gc.ca/eau-water/default.asp?lang=En&n=F25C70EC-1

32. Free The Children, www.freethechildren.com/whatwedo/international/aav/water/

33. Blue Planet Network, www.blueplanetnetwork.org/water/facts

34. Bikes Belong, www.bikesbelong.org/resources/stats-and-research/statistics/health-statistics/

35. United Nations Millennium Development Goals, www.un.org/millenniumgoals/poverty.shtml

36. Aboriginal Affairs and Northern Development Canada: www.aadnc-aandc.gc.ca/eng/1302807151028/1302807416851

37. *ScienceDaily*, www.sciencedaily.com/releases/2007/07/070702161141.htm

38. Gamespot, www.gamespot.com/news/time-spent-gaming-on-the-rise-npd-6264092

39. The last one is strictly from personal experience.

40. The Elders, www.theelders.org/child-marriage/about-child-marriage

41. Tree Hugger, www.treehugger.com/travel/air-travel-and-climate-change-take-the-train.html

42. Environment Canada, www.climate.weatheroffice.gc.ca/winners/winners_e.html

43. The Canadian Encyclopedia, www.thecanadianencyclopedia.com/articles/nordicity

44. *The World Bank*, http://siteresources.worldbank.org/JAPANINJAPANESEEXT/Resources/515497-1201490097949/080827_The_Developing_World_is_Poorer_than_we_Thought.pdf

45. If such a school existed, that would be Foo-Fightery awesome. We were going to say "that would be nirvana" but that's both cheesy and unlikely to be understood by casual Foo Fighter fans.

46. ASSIST, www.assistgroup.ca/

47. Friends of the Earth, http://action.foe.org/content.jsp?content_KEY=3018&t=2007_Ships.dwt

48. We're assuming an eight-hour workday with no one going in the first hour of work, or the first hour after lunch, which means five hours, or 60 five-minute windows of potential coincidental pee time, times two for the two sexes. But stats never was our strongest course.

49. *Macleans,* http://www2.macleans.ca/2009/12/08/where-to-draw-the-line-on-child-poverty/

50. National Centre for Biotechnology Information, www.ncbi.nlm.nih.gov/pmc/articles/PMC1964887/

51. The average Canadian family consumes 360 litres of water a day, of which 220 litres are hot water: Hydro One, www.hydroone.com/MyHome/SaveEnergy/Documents/Conserving_Energy_UsingHotWater.pdf.

There are roughly 11 million Canadian families (34 million divided by approximately 3 members per family): Statistics Canada, www.statcan.gc.ca/tables-tableaux/sum-som/l01/cst01/famil40-eng.htm, and an Olympic-sized swimming pool contains approximately 2.5 million litres of water.

52. University of Alberta, www.ualberta.ca/~cbeedac/publications/documents/domwater_000.pdf

53. *The Economist: Intelligence Unit Report*, http://viewswire.eiu.com/index.asp?layout=VWPrintVW3&article_id=568674641&printer=printer

54. *The Toronto Star*, http://www.healthzone.ca/health/articlePrint/429617. That's more than 210 million kg of food, in case you were wondering how much 35,000 African elephants weigh.

55. Natural Resource Defense Council, www.nrdc.org/onearth/04fal/livgreen.asp; *Joyous Health*, www.joyoushealth.ca/2011/04/23/12-dirty-chemicals-in-your-personal-care-products/ *The Globe and Mail*, http://eha-ab.ca/news/articles/GlobeAndMail2010-04-10.pdf

56. Coconut oil is a great moisturizer and make-up remover, a half-cup of baking soda is a fab skin-smoothening alternative to bath oils, and a sprinkle of corn starch solves oily morning hair.

57. Earth Share, www.earthshare.org/2008/09/windows-and-ene.html

58. Natural Resources Canada has great resources for keeping the heat in: http://oee.nrcan.gc.ca/publications/residential/8584

59. International Labour Organization, www.ilo.org/global/topics/forced-labour/lang--en/index.htm

60. Environment Canada, www.ec.gc.ca/dd-sd/default.asp?lang=En&n=16AF9508-1

61. International Energy Agency, www.iea.org/newsroomandevents/news/2012/june/name,27722,en.html

62. *CBC*, www.cbc.ca/news/yourcommunity/2011/11/which-do-you-prefer-traditional-or-electronic-greeting-cards.html

63. The purchase of each Me to We card provides a specific benefit to help end poverty around the world, including:

- planting a tree
- inoculating an infant
- a source of clean water
- school supplies
- school lunches

Greetings cards available for individual purchase or discount bulk orders. www.metowe.com/cards

64. CNN: The CNN Freedom Project, http://thecnnfreedomproject.blogs.cnn.com/2011/09/19/the-human-cost-of-chocolate/

65. Set up your viewing for Dark Side of Chocolate through the International Labour Rights Forum at: https://afl.salsalabs.com/o/4058/donate_page/darkside

66. Earth Day Canada, www.earthday.ca/giveitup/toxic_cleaners.php

67. Three more recipes for cleaning:

- Carpet cleaner: Mix equal parts white vinegar and water in a spray bottle. Spray directly on stain, let sit for several minutes, and clean with a brush or sponge using warm soapy water. For fresh grease spots on your carpet, sprinkle corn starch onto spot and wait 15 - 30 minutes before vacuuming. (http://eartheasy.com/live_nontoxic_solutions.htm)

- Air fresheners: Place baking soda or vinegar with lemon juice in small dishes around the house to absorb odours. (http://eartheasy.com/live_nontoxic_solutions.htm)

- Oven Cleaner: Moisten oven surfaces with sponge and water. Use 3/4 cup baking soda, 1/4 cup salt and 1/4 cup water to make a thick paste, and spread throughout oven interior (avoid bare metal and any openings). Let sit overnight. Remove with spatula and wipe clean. Rub gently with fine steel wool for tough spots. (http://eartheasy.com/live_nontoxic_solutions.htm)

- A great all-purpose cleaning spray for mirrors, windows and counters is 2:1 water to white vinegar.

68. Canadian Newswire, www.newswire.ca/en/story/654369/canadians-say-yes-to-ethical-gift-giving-for-the-holidays-plan-survey

69. Island Parent, www.islandparent.ca/family/wantnot.html

70. Shawn Achor: The happy secret to better work, www.ted.com/talks/shawn_achor_the_happy_secret_to_better_work.html

71. World Bank ABCDE Conference, www.tanzaniagateway.org/docs/sustainable_tourism_and_poverty_alleviation.pdf

72. *The Toronto Star*, www.thestar.com/news/insight/article/654217--a-strawberry-s-journey-from-west-to-feast

73. Find your local farmers' market at www.farmersmarketscanada.ca.

74. Find your local CSA at http://usc-canada.org/storyoffood/what-you-can-do.

75. DeskMag, www.deskmag.com/en/first-results-of-global-coworking-survey-171

76. BC Hydro, www.bchydro.com/guides_tips/green-your-home/heating_guide/manage_thermostat.html. World Wildlife Fund, http://assets.wwf.ca/downloads/sweaterday_toolkit_schools.pdf

77. Okay, we made this stat up, but judging by us and our friends growing up, it's probably close, no?

78. College of Education and Human Development, University of Minnesota, www.cehd.umn.edu/research/highlights/Rossmann/

79. Car Sharing Canada, http://autoshare.com/ca/clean_and_green.html

80. Car Sharing Canada, http://autoshare.com/ca/how_it_works.html

81. Global Issues, www.globalissues.org/article/26/poverty-facts-and-stats

82. Mashable Tech, http://mashable.com/2011/11/09/tech-germs/

83. *PC World*, www.pcworld.com/article/153245/unplug_for_dollars_stop_vampire_power_waste.html#75 after messages a day TechVibes. http://www.techvibes.com/blog/canadians-exchange-220-million-texts-per-day-as-sms-usage-continues-to-grow-2011-09-26

84. *TechVibes*, www.techvibes.com/blog/canadians-exchange-220-million-texts-per-day-as-sms-usage-continues-to-grow-2011-09-26

85. EcoHearth, http://ecohearth.com/eco-blogs/guest-blog/58-10-easy-eco-steps-to-take-now.html

86. The latest statistics accessed were for April 2012, when 1.37 million Canadians were unemployed (www.statcan.gc.ca/daily-quotidien/120511/t120511a001-eng.htm) and annualized for 2011 (1.39 million) (www.statcan.gc.ca/tables-tableaux/sum-som/l01/cst01/labor07a-eng.htm). The youth statistic was 13.9 % unemployment (www.statcan.gc.ca/daily-quotidien/120511/t120511a001-eng.htm).

87. Water Aid America, www.wateraidamerica.org/includes/documents/cm_docs/2008/w/women_and_wateraid_2006.pdf)

88. Free The Children, www.freethechildren.com/adoptavillage/

89. Natural Resources Canada: Canada's dryers: 7.2 billion kWh http://oee.nrcan.gc.ca/equipment/appliance/10517; CIA World Factbook: Guatemala: 7.1 billion kWh for 14 million people, and Kenya: 5.7 billion kWh for 41 million people www.cia.gov/library/publications/the-world-factbook/rankorder/2042rank.html

90. Shopbot (according to rates in 2012) between $325 and $900 retail, www.shopbot.ca/clothes-dryers/home-appliances/canada/1069, between $520 and $1,150 in electricity costs over 18 years (912 kWh/year at 7 cents per kWh for standard dryers, 413 kWh/year for compact dryers), Natural Resources Canada, http://oee.nrcan.gc.ca/equipment/manufacturers/15660

Canadian Tire (according to rates in 2012), www.canadiantire.ca/AST/browse/3/HouseHome/Laundry/IndoorOutdoorDryers.jsp?locale=en

91. InnoVisions Canada/Canadian Telework Association, www.ivc.ca/cleanair/index.htm; David Suzuki Foundation, www.davidsuzuki.org/what-you-can-do/reduce-your-carbon-footprint/

92. *Canadian Business Journal*, www.cbj.ca/blog/here-comes-the-bill/

93. Likely.

94. Me to We Trips, www.metowe.com/trips, offers volunteer trip opportunities for youth, families, school groups, corporate groups, and individual adults.

Also, please see page 145 of this book for more information on volunteer travel opportunities.

95. Harvard Faculty of Arts and Sciences, www.fas.harvard.edu/home/news-and-notices/news/press-releases/endurance-04192010.shtml.

96. The last part about being a jerk wasn't in the Harvard study, but is fairly self-evident, we think.

97. The Wellesley Institute, www.wellesleyinstitute.com/wp-content/uploads/2012/02/Precarious-Housing-Flip-Sheet.pdf

98. Sleep Country Canada, www.sleepcountry.ca/aboutus/charities.aspx

99. *CBC*, www.cbc.ca/news/polls/canada-world/adams-results.html;

The Globe and Mail, www.theglobeandmail.com/news/politics/ottawa-notebook/what-will-it-take-to-win-over-the-apathetic-85-per-cent-of-voters/article611243/

100. Okay, so we made that one up

101. DM Depot, www.dmdepot.ca/(for Blackberry). iRepair.ca, www.irepair.ca (for iPhone, iPod and iPad repair)

Cell Phone Repair Canada, www.cellphonerepaircanada.com/cell_phone_repair.html (for iPhone, BlackBerry and Android)

102. Daily Mail, www.dailymail.co.uk/travel/article-588019/Not-getting-air-mileage.html

ABOUT FREE THE CHILDREN

Photo courtesy of V. Tony Hauser

FREE THE CHILDREN

Free The Children is an international charity and educational partner. Domestically through We Day and We Act, we educate, engage and empower youth to become active citizens. Internationally, our sustainable development model, Adopt a Village, removes barriers to education and empowers communities to break the cycle of poverty.

Get involved with Free The Children:

- Donate. $25 gives one person clean water for life; $8,500 builds a classroom.

- Support one of our five development pillars such as building a school or water project for a village.

- Adopt an entire village. Fundraise for all five pillars, and help transform a whole community.

Visit **www.freethechildren.com** to find out more.

ABOUT WE DAY

WE DAY ›WE ACT

We Day is a series of stadium-sized events that celebrate the power of youth to create positive change in their local and global communities. Youth can't buy a ticket to We Day – they earn it through service.

We Act is a comprehensive service learning program that empowers schools and youth groups to take at least one local and one global action. In turn, schools and groups receive mentor support, educational tools and resources to make their We Act commitments come to life.

Through We Day and We Act:

- 2 million young people from around the world take part in programs and campaigns

- 4 million pounds of food has been collected for local food banks

- 6 million hours have been volunteered for local and global causes

- $32 million has been raised for more than 1,000 local and global causes

Visit **www.weday.com** to learn more and to sign up for We Act.

ABOUT WE 365

WE 365

We365 is where people live the spirit of We Day—365 days of the year.

This mobile application and website empowers youth to create a portfolio of their social impact, while connecting with friends and classmates to create a community that is centred on actions for social good. Free to join, We365 is the online community for anyone looking to turn their passion into action.On this platform, young people can:

- Build a social impact portfolio
- Track and verify volunteer hours
- Fundraise for any charity
- Discover, join, and create service actions
- Organize class and community group campaigns
- Explore inspiring, educational content on social issues
- Compliment college and university and scholarship applications

Visit **www.We365.com** to join.

ABOUT ME TO WE

ME
TO
WE

Me to We is an innovative social enterprise that provides people with better choices for a better world, and measures the bottom line by the number of lives we change. Half of Me to We's net profit is donated to Free The Children and the other half is reinvested to grow the enterprise.

Embrace Me to We:

- Experience life-changing volunteer trips around the world.

- Wear Me to We Artisans, accessories with a purpose.

- Sport Me to We Style, domestically produced, sweatshop-free clothing.

- Exercise choice with socially conscious and environmentally friendly products.

Visit **www.metowe.com** to find out more.

GET INSPIRED BY OUR AMAZING SPEAKERS

Me to We Speakers offers the most inspirational people with remarkable stories and life experiences. From community activists to social entrepreneurs, our roster of energetic, experienced speakers are leading the Me to We movement: living and working in developing communities, helping businesses achieve social responsibility and inspiring auditoriums of youth and educators to action.

They'll make you laugh, cry and gain a new perspective on what really matters. Be warned: their passion is contagious!

Visit **www.metowe.com/speakers** to learn more.

TRAVEL WITH US TO AFRICA, ASIA OR LATIN AMERICA

Interested in a volunteer travel experience that changes your perspective, while positively transforming the lives of others?

On a Me to We trip, you will help build schools, teach heartwarming children and discover age-old cultures. The experience provides a deeper sense of gratitude about life's simple blessings.

Our staff welcomes you into the communities where they live and work. In complete safety and comfort, more than 3,000 adventurous people of all ages have chosen to volunteer abroad with us. We welcome youth, families and groups.

Visit **www.metowe.com/trips** to learn more.

BOOKS WITH A REAL MESSAGE

Me to We
Craig and Marc Kielburger

Me to We is a manual, a manifesto and a movement. It's about finding meaning in our lives and our world by reaching out to others. In this book, Craig and Marc Kielburger share their knowledge, complimented and reinforced by contributors like Richard Gere, Dr. Jane Goodall, Her Majesty Queen Noor and Oprah Winfrey.

Free the Children
Craig Kielburger

This is the story that launched a movement. *Free the Children* recounts 12-year-old Craig Kielburger's remarkable odyssey across South Asia, meeting some of the world's most disadvantaged children, exploring slums and sweatshops and fighting to rescue children from the chains of inhumane conditions.

Living Me to We
Craig and Marc Kielburger

We all want to make a difference. Now it's easier to lead a life that makes the world a better place every day. With this specifically Canadian guide, readers are provided tips from morning to bedtime. Contributions from your favorite Canadians, such as Margaret Atwood and Rick Hanson.

The World Needs Your Kid
Craig and Marc Kielburger
and Shelley Page

This unique guide to parenting advances the philosophy of the three C's: compassion, courage, and community, which encourage children to become global citizens. The book draws on life lessons from remarkable individuals like Elie Wiesel and Archbishop Desmond Tutu.

Global Voices, The Compilation: Vol. 1
Craig and Marc Kielburger

Global Voices aims to tell the untold stories of people and issues from around the world. This book will inspire young readers to deepen their understanding of issues and explore how they can change these headlines.

Standing Tall
Spencer West

Navigating life on his hands, Spencer has always lived with purpose. This is the candid, coming-of-age story of a young man's journey of working hard, laughing a lot and always standing tall.

My Maasai Life
Robin Wiszowaty

In her early 20s, Robin Wiszowaty left the ordinary world behind to join a traditional Maasai family. With full-colour photographs from her adventures, Robin's heart-wrenching story will inspire you to question your own definitions of home, happiness and family.

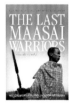

The Last Maasai Warriors
Wilson Meikuaya and Jackson Ntirkana

Wilson and Jackson are brave warriors of the Maasai, an intensely proud culture built on countless generations steeped in the mystique of tradition, legend and prophecy. They represent the final generation to literally fight for their way of life—they are the last of the great warriors.

BOOKS WITH A REAL MESSAGE FOR YOUNGER READERS

Everyone's Birthday
Marc Kielburger

A birthday celebration in Thailand changes the course of a young Marc Kielburger's life. With full-colour illustrations follow Marc in this true story about discovering the importance of celebrating life's many blessings.

Lessons from a Street Kid
Craig Kielburger

It was on the streets of Brazil that Craig learned firsthand a lesson in generosity from street children. This full-colour illustrated children's book teaches that we all have gifts to share.

My Maasai Life: A Child's Adventure in Kenya
Robin Wiszowaty

Follow a young Robin Wiszowaty on the adventure of a lifetime, living among Maasai on her first visit to Kenya.
In this true story, crafted for children and with full-colour illustrations, Robin explores the land and culture of the Maasai Mara — a place she would one day call home.

Visit **www.metowe.com/books** to see our full list of bestselling books.

The Buy a Book, Give a Book promise ensures that for every Me to We book purchased, a notebook will be given to a child in a developing country.

STAY CONNECTED WITH ME TO WE

we365.com

twitter.com/realmetowe

facebook.com/metowe

Go to **www.metowe.com** to start living *me* to *we* today.